Introduction

Of all the pets that you might choose to keep in your home as a companion, the little guinea pig, or cavy, as it is also known, must rank among the best. It is large enough to be handled and petted, yet small enough to be accommodated without any problems. It has no characteristic body odor and is exceptionally clean in its personal habits (but, in fairness, so are all rodents—yes, including mice and rats!). Cavies are simplicity itself to feed, and they are quiet pets whose little squeaks are endearing rather than annoying, as can be the case with dogs, cats, or parrots.

To round off the benefits of guinea pigs, they are very modestly priced and come in a range of colors, patterns, and coat types to suit all tastes. While not especially long-lived compared to dogs, cats, and parrots, they may attain seven or even eight years of age, which is a much longer lifespan potential than any other popular pet rodent other than the chinchilla.

◄ When fully grown, a guinea pig will weigh between one and three pounds and will be about eight to ten inches long.

What is a Guinea Pig?

The guinea pig is a member of the order of mammals known as Rodentia. This is the largest and most successful of any mammalian order and contains 40% of all mammals. Rodents are found pretty much all over the world—where they were not indigenous they have been introduced by us. The most striking feature of rodents is their paired incisor teeth, which are designed to chisel and gnaw. These teeth grow continually throughout the life of the animal and are kept in trim by grinding against each other and against hard objects—grain, tree bark, and so on.

Guinea pigs can make wonderful pets. They're cute, hardy, and have endearing personalities. ◄

1

Guinea pigs come in a number of colors and coat types. There is something for everyone.

Cavies form a family of their own, which is called Caviidae. All guinea pig species are native to South America.

They live in family units of up to 15, which comprise a boar, a sow, and their offspring of one or two generations. Some guinea pigs live in burrows while others live on open ground and take cover under bushes and grasses as a means of shelter. Our little pet guinea pig is of this type and is crepuscular (active at dawn and dusk), rather than totally nocturnal, in its habits—as are many of its relatives.

A cream guinea pig.

The Domestic, or Pet, Guinea Pig

As with most other popular pets, the full domestic history of the guinea pig was never recorded. It is thought that the South American Indians kept and bred these little rodents as a source of meat as long ago as 3,000 BC. However, not until the arrival of the Spanish conquistadors during the 16th century did western eyes come to know and appreciate this furry bundle with no tail.

Even today, no one is sure whether the guinea pig is a domesticated wild species or a variant bred from one or more wild species. It is usually designated in zoological circles with the scientific name of *Cavia porcellus*. However, some authorities believe it is actually derived from *C. aperea, C. tschudii,* or *C.*

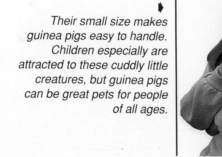

Their small size makes guinea pigs easy to handle. Children especially are attracted to these cuddly little creatures, but guinea pigs can be great pets for people of all ages.

fulgida. Interestingly, the variation noted in such matters as gestation periods, litter size, and birth weights in domestic guinea pigs could suggest a mixed species origin.

Be these matters as they may, the arrival of the guinea pig in Europe firmly established it as a popular pet among the wealthy. With the passage of time, it filtered down to the working class. As it gained in numbers, mutations started to appear. These mutations merely increased interest in the guinea pig, and it has steadily gained friends the world over. It has, of course, been used extensively as a laboratory specimen—so much so that the term "guinea pig" is synonymous with experimental, or first time, try-outs in everyday life. The question of how it came to be known as a

guinea pig in the first place is speculative. Some think that Spanish ships stopped at African ports en route back to Spain. The fact that they visited ports in Guinea may have prompted people to think that is where the animals originated. The term "pig" may have derived from the pig-like squeals made by these pets when they are alarmed or excited. Then again, some say the price of one of these pets in England was a golden guinea—a princely sum in years gone by.

In the following chapters of this book, you will be guided through all stages of obtaining, caring for, and breeding these fascinating little pets.

← This youngster is getting acquainted with her new pet guinea pigs. When you bring your new pet home, give it time to settle down: don't overhandle the animal.

◀ Guinea pigs that have coats of one solid color are known as selfs.

→ A young Abyssinian guinea pig. This breed is distinguished by rosettes, or whorls, on the coat. In a good specimen, the rosettes will be round and very distinct.

Accommodations

There are three types of housing that are used for guinea pigs, depending on the reasons the guinea pigs are being kept: 1) wire cages, either as single or multiple units, 2) rabbit-style hutches of various sizes, 3) open-box-type pens. In the past, breeders traditionally chose rabbit-style hutches simply because they were convenient and available in a variety of sizes. More recently, however, they have been opting for wire cages because they are more hygienic and less expensive than wooden cages. Laboratories have always used wire cages because they represent the optimum in hygiene potential.

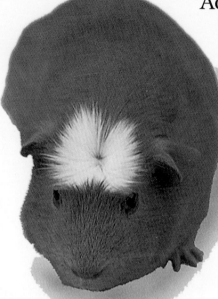

◆ A White Crested American guinea pig.

◆ Guinea pigs do not need to be bathed on a regular basis. Only when your pet has gotten really dirty should it be bathed.

A variety of bedding materials: hay, straw, and wood shavings.

All-Wire Cages

Wire cages have their advantages and disadvantages. Being easy to see out of, the guinea pig does not so readily panic as it may do in an enclosed unit. On the other hand, it is essential that the floor has a very small hole-size. Otherwise, the tiny feet of these pets, and especially the long nails, can easily get caught—with resulting leg injuries. The hole size of the floor should be no more than 10mm (⅜ in.) and should ideally be covered with a number of paper sheets topped with a generous layer of wood shavings. If the cage is in a stacked-unit form, it should be fitted with a sliding solid-floor tray. While wire cages do have obvious practical advantages, it must be remembered that they were designed to house these pets for only short periods in research institutes. From a pet perspective, where long life of the pet is anticipated, it would be wise to feature a wooden floor over the wire base. This will be much more comfortable for the pet. These cages are made in a number of styles and sizes. Ideally, they should be chromium plated because normal galvanized wire is not easily kept in a really clean state.

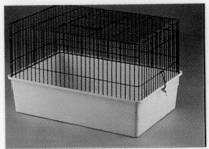

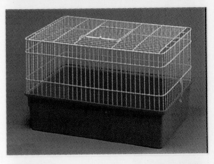

◀ *It is best to purchase the cage and all of its accessories before you acquire your guinea pig. This will help to make the animal's transition into your home a smooth one.*

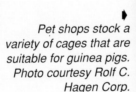

▶
Pet shops stock a variety of cages that are suitable for guinea pigs. Photo courtesy Rolf C. Hagen Corp.

Wooden Hutches

Your petshop may sell small rabbit hutches, which will be just fine for one or two guinea pigs. You will get what you pay for. If you are looking for low-cost accommodations, they will be made of low-cost materials that will have a minimal life when compared to stoutly made hutches. It is therefore best to purchase hutches made of solid timbers rather than those made of plywood. (Plywood hutches are totally unsuitable for outdoor use.)

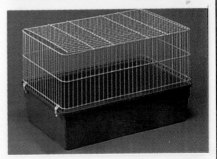

You should regard the *minimum* size for one or two pets as being 62x31x31cm (24x12x12 in.), assuming you are allowing your pet plenty of exercise room outside of its cage. Guinea pigs are very active little pets and really do enjoy scampering about. Commercially made hutches are usually sold unpainted and should be given a few coats of paint to make cleaning easier. If you fit a false floor that has been painted, it will provide better protection to the floor from spilt water and urine. Such a floor can be replaced periodically.

Open-Box-Type Pens

There may be some exceptions, but, as a rule, guinea pigs are neither good climbers nor jumpers, which means they can be housed in open-box-type pens. For the in-house pet, such units are excellent. The walls of the pen need be no more than 15cm (6 in.) high. They can be of weldwire or of wood. The floor should be made of stout (say 1.25cm (12 in.)) timber that has been well painted. A nesting box can be placed into this pen and will provide a cozy retreat for your pet to sleep in. The size of the pen should be as large as space will permit in order to provide ample exercise room in it. If you have other pets, such as a dog or a cat, it would be prudent to cover the top of the pen with 2.5cm (1 in.) or smaller hole size weldwire of 19 or lower gauge and turn it over the edges of the pen so it is a secure fit. You might place the weldwire on a wooden frame that is hinged to the pen, and in this way you can easily open it to attend to chores and to lift out your pet.

Longhaired guinea pigs need regular attention to their coats to prevent mats and tangles.

This portable outdoor enclosure allows its occupants to nibble on the grass. It also has a sheltered area, to which the animals can retreat should the weather suddenly turn inclement.

A child can actively participate in caring for the family guinea pig.

Floor Covering

Although sawdust has a high absorbency capacity, I would not recommend its use with these animals. For one thing, it can cause irritation to their eyes. It can also negatively affect breeding performance because it can irritate the vulva of the sow and the prepuce (foreskin) of the boar's penis. Further, it has a tendency to cling to moist mashes and fresh foods. A better choice would be a good layer of wood shavings over a few layers of newspaper or brown paper (which will not stain light-colored guinea pigs with newsprint if it gets wet).

Another alternative is the new kind of cat litter that is made of natural plant-matter granules. Granulated paper also can be used. It, too, has a high absorbency without presenting the risk of causing irritation. Hay is, of course, an excellent top dressing because it is both warm and a good food source rich in fiber. But it should be very fresh, dry, and free of mold, which can cause all kinds of problems for your pet. You can, of course, purchase meadow hay from feed stores, but it is much better to buy prepacked hay, sold in pet shops, that has been selected for its quality.

Food and Water Containers

In order that your pet does not tip over its food bowl, it is best to use food bowls made of crock

▲ These guinea pigs are enjoying a meal of fresh greens and dry food. Any greens that are to be served to your pet should first be washed to rid them of any pesticides.

➡ Plastic bowls such as this are not recommended for guinea pigs because they are easily tipped.

7

← If you want to let your guinea pig roam free in certain areas of your home, you must first take precautions against any safety hazards, e.g., electrical cords.

(earthenware). You can buy these bowls, which come in different sizes, in your pet shop. The kind used for a rabbit or a cat will be suitable. You will need one bowl for dry food and one for moist mashes and greenfoods. Water is best given via gravity-fed water bottles, which come in various sizes. Purchase the more costly kind, as they will not so readily start to drip, which can be a nuisance. If you have a breeding room, you can equip it with an automatic watering system, which comes in various designs.

Location of the Accommodations

Guinea pigs can tolerate a wide range of temperatures, but they are not able to cope with rapid temperature fluctuations or dampness. They are probably best kept within the range of 60 to 70°F (15.6 to 21°C). Do not place their cage opposite doors or close to radiators that are alternately switching on and off.

← Any greenfoods that you serve your pet should be fresh and of good quality.

← A pair of pet-quality guinea pigs.

Also, be sure that the cage is not placed in such a way that it is receiving direct sunlight for long periods of the day. Your pet should always be able to easily retreat from direct sunlight. If it cannot, it will become stressed, as it will if it is subjected to a lot of sudden noises and activity. Being high-strung animals, guinea pigs are more prone to stress-related problems than are many other small animals. The breeder also should be aware that guinea pigs cannot tolerate high ammonia levels and are very susceptible to them, even at relatively low levels. Ammonia is released via the urine. Apart from regular cleaning of the accommodations, the best way to minimize ammonia levels is to ensure that the stock room is adequately ventilated—but not drafty.

Selection

In your excitement to rush out and purchase your first guinea pig, it is very possible that you could end up with a pet that is not quite what you really wanted. It is altogether better to go about the process based on your exact needs. There are four "whats" that you need to consider: what age, what sex, what breed, and what color? Actually, you could add a fifth—what for? Apart from these questions, you must, of course, be sure that your

A young Himalayan-marked guinea pig. As with many other kinds of pets, many people want to start out with a young guinea pig so that they can enjoy it for as long as possible.

◀ When choosing your guinea pig, the most important factor to be considered is the health of the animal.

new pet is very healthy. Otherwise, your enjoyment will be ruined from the minute your pet arrives in your home.

What Age?

The pet owner should obtain a young guinea pig, both to enjoy having it as a pet for a longer period, and because it will be easier to make it nice and tame. These pets are weaned from their mother's milk within the period of 21-30 days of age, although they will have been eating solid foods almost from the time they were born. Unlike most other pets that you may be

➤ A tortoiseshell-and-white guinea pig. There are four toes on the guinea pig's front feet, and there are three toes on the guinea pig's back feet.

⬆ Sexing a guinea pig. This is a male, as evidenced by the penis protruding from the y-shaped slit.

⬆ A healthy guinea pig will be bright eyed, alert, and interested in its surroundings.

If you have other household pets, you must take precautions so that they do not frighten or harm your guinea pig. ▶

Sexing a guinea pig. This is a female. ⬆

familiar with, guinea pigs are born fully furred with their eyes open and are running around within hours of their birth. Four weeks of age, or within a few weeks of this age, is a good age for a pet. However, even a young adult can be a nice pet if it is not excessively nervous and hand shy.

What Sex?

If you plan to keep only an individual pet, then either sex will be fine. Boars will normally be somewhat larger than sows, but size is also influenced by genetic background, so a sow can be larger than a boar. Both are very clean animals, so gender need not be a major consideration—just obtain the one that meets your other needs.

Sexing very young guinea pigs is not always easy. By restraining them on their backs in the palm of your hand, you can apply digital pressure to the ano-genital orifice, where the penis of the male can be extruded. The sow normally has just one pair of nipples.

If you want to keep two guinea pigs together, then females should be chosen. They will get on well with each other. Two males will, sooner or later, start to fight and can inflict serious injuries on each other. Boars will never attack females, so you can run a male with one or a number of females without any problems—depending on whether you regard the arrival of babies as a problem!

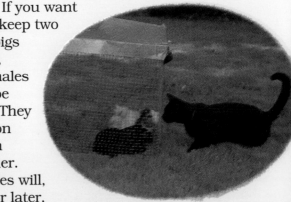

Guinea pig mothers normally do not have large litters, so that if a sow produces a litter, it is

→ *Whether shorthaired or longhaired, a guinea pig's coat should not exhibit any bald spots.*

unlikely you will have problems locating good homes for the youngsters. In rabbits, mice, and gerbils, casual breeding can cause the owner a dilemma because of the high number of offspring.

What Breed?

The choice of breed should be made with plenty of thought. This is especially so if you fancy owning a Peruvian or a Silkie (Sheltie). They are longcoated breeds. Their fur can be the source of many problems, both in day-to-day management, and when they are used for breeding. A long coat quickly picks up dust, shavings, hay, and other kinds of debris. If it is not groomed daily, it will very soon become a mass of tangles and mats. This will make life very unpleasant for your pet. As a general rule, you should make your first guinea pig an American, a Crested, or an Abyssinian, all of which have easily managed coats.

▲ *Males and females make equally good pets.*

What Color?

Each of the breeds is available in a very impressive range of colors and patterns. No pet shop can possibly stock all of the colors/patterns that are seen in guinea pigs, so if you don't see kind that you want, talk to the pet shop dealer. It is possible that he can order the specific guinea pig that you want.

→ *In general, sows are a bit smaller than boars, but there are exceptions to this rule.*

◀ *Shorthaired guinea pigs, like this American, require the simplest of grooming regimens.*

◆ *Guinea pigs have poor vision, but their sense of hearing is good.*

◆ *Guinea pigs have padding on their feet. When they want to, they can move around with surprising speed.*

▸
Guinea pigs have the smallest litters of all rodents. A first-time litter will average two to three babies; subsequent litters will average four to six babies.

What For?

The reasons why you want the guinea pig will have a considerable bearing on the quality of animal you must purchase. The least expensive guinea pig will be the everyday pet. The breeding or show-quality individual is going to be rather more costly, depending specifically on its level of quality and whether it has won at shows and/or bred some fine offspring. For such a guinea pig, you will need to be familiar with the standard for its breed. (If you have the opportunity to attend a guinea pig show, you will see what a quality guinea pig is all about.)

The Matter of Health

Having made a determination on all of the other factors discussed, your final consideration is knowing how to select a healthy individual. The process starts by your careful observation of the conditions under which the guinea pigs are living. It follows that if they are dirty and overcrowded, the chances are high that the stock will not be in the best of health, so a new source of supply should be found. A good pet shop will not offer for sale anything but very healthy guinea pigs, which will be housed under nice clean conditions. Even so, you need to know how to spot a guinea pig that is not well, or one that has a problem—even if it is not life threatening.

Watch the guinea pigs as they move about. Do not select any that show a sign of impediment in their movement. Such a condition may be only a temporary strain, but then again it may be a permanent limp. If a guinea pig sits hunched in a corner with its fur standing away from its lie, you can assume it is not feeling well. Unfortunately, if just one such guinea pig is displaying signs of ill health, you must work on the premise that the others have been exposed to the problem and may come down with it over the next few days.

A fit specimen will have a nice sheen to its coat. Its eyes will be sparkling and fully open, and it will be very alert to all that is going on around it. There will be no bald patches and no signs of weeping eyes or runny nose. The anal region will be clean

Guinea pigs are clean animals. They are practically odorless and groom themselves much in the same way as do cats.

and not stained from diarrhea or caked with hard fecal matter. There will be no lumps, sores, or other abrasions on any part of the skin. By brushing the fur of the rump against its lie, you can inspect the skin for parasites or signs of their fecal matter. The fur should spring back when released. Dull-looking fur is not a good sign.

There should be four toes on the front feet and three on the rear. This is vital in a show specimen, and anything other than this is an automatic disqualification. An extra or missing toe will not unduly bother a pet, but the animal should not be used for breeding.

The legs of a guinea pig are quite short in relation to the length of the body.

Grooming time for this Peruvian guinea pig. With a longhaired breed, a grooming regimen should be started when the animal is young.

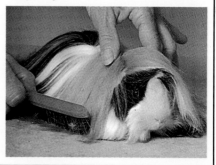

A gravity-fed water bottle. This is the best way to supply your guinea pig with water. Photo courtesy Rolf C. Hagen Corp.

Feeding

Guinea pigs, like all other rodents, are extremely easy to care for in their nutritional requirements. This said, there are a few important aspects that should always be kept in mind. We will discuss them before looking at a typical feeding regimen.

General Feeding Comments

Guinea pigs, like primates (monkeys and humans), cannot synthesize vitamin C (ascorbic acid) as can all other mammals. This means that vitamin C must be present in their diets in sufficient quantity to ensure that an adequate amount is ingested. If it is not, their health will definitely suffer, and the response of their immune system will also be negatively affected.

Although the nutritional needs of guinea pigs are still not completely understood, it is thought that a lack of fiber in the diet will be deleterious to their health, especially if they are in a stress situation. This being so, prepared commercial diets will need to be supplemented with ample hay, green vegetables, and foods such as carrots. Another point that is

Guinea pigs love greens. However, such items should be considered as a supplement to the main diet, which should consist of pelleted food specially formulated for guinea pigs.

sometimes overlooked is that if foods are stored for more than 60 days, their vitamin content will steadily decline. If, for cost-effective reasons, breeders buy hay and dry food in bulk, they should consider a vitamin supplement, under veterinary advice, to compensate for any vitamins that are lost in these foods as they age. All greenfoods and fruit must be fit for human consumption if they are to be given to guinea pigs. They should be rinsed before being fed in order to remove any residual chemicals with which they may have been sprayed. Any moist mash foods prepared in advance and stored in the freezer must be fully thawed before being given to your pet. Clean drinking water should be available at all times.

▲ Lettuce is one greenfood that has little nutritional value. Additionally, if it is fed in excessive amounts, it can cause problems in the digestive tract.

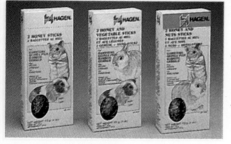

◀ Your pet shop dealer can recommend a variety of foods that your guinea pig will enjoy. Photo courtesy Rolf C. Hagen Corp.

☛ Commercially prepared food products make it easy for you to provide your pet with a nutritionally balanced diet. Photo courtesy Rolf C. Hagen Corp.

The Typical Diet

Your pet's diet can be broadly divided into two basic categories: dry food and fresh foods. The dry foods will comprise either prepackaged pet-shop mixes, commercially made mixes, or mixes that you have prepared from the various possible ingredients. These ingredients will normally include crushed oats, maize, wheat, barley, bran, and similar cereal crops. Larger seeds, such as sunflower, may also be included, along with unsalted peanuts. Wholemeal bread, dog biscuits, and unsweetened whole-grain breakfast cereals can also be added to the menu and will provide extra gnawing foods.

Fresh foods include vegetables such as carrots, cabbage, celery, cress, peas, and beans. Your pet

An Abyssinian guinea pig. Note the nice glossy quality of the coat.

Pelleted food specially formulated for guinea pigs is available at most pet shops. Photo courtesy Rolf C. Hagen.

A good diet will be reflected in your pet's overall appearance.

will exhibit preferences for some foods more than others. Wild plants are much enjoyed. They include dandelion, chickweed, bramble, yarrow, plantain, and clover. With regard to wild plants, follow the comment, "If in doubt, leave it out." Fruits like apples, grapes, and oranges may be taken with varying degrees of relish, according to appetite. Avoid feeding sweetened foods and, of course, any that you would regard as "junk foods." Guinea pigs are not meat eaters, although in the wild they will consume certain invertebrates (worms, beetles, etc).

Mashes

You can prepare dry or moist mashes to provide a change from your normal presentation of foods. A moist mash can have something like porridge oats or even boiled potatoes as a base ingredient to provide consistency to the mash. Then you can add a range of the foods previously discussed. Be sure that they are finely minced. You can also add beef extract and chopped hard-boiled eggs to provide extra protein content. The mash can be just dampened with the beef extract, soup, or warm water.

How Much To Feed?

The amount of food needed by your pet(s) is determined by many factors, such as individual metabolism, ambient environmental temperature, age, breeding status (such as a nursing sow), and the extent of exercise given. By trial and error, you can quickly find out what each guinea pig needs and likes. Dry foods can be supplied on an ad lib basis and will be consumed steadily over any 24-hour period. Fresh foods and moist mashes have a much more limited feeding life, so give them in small quantities early in the morning or later in the day and take note of how much is eaten at a single sitting.

Breeding and Exhibition

The breeding of any animal is not something that you should contemplate until you have gained some practical experience in keeping that animal. As experience is gained, you are better able to judge whether the whole idea of breeding still appeals to you. At the same time, it gives you the opportunity to plan ahead, to decide which varieties you wish to keep, and to prepare the extra housing that will be needed for the increasing numbers of young stock that you will retain.

◆ Guinea pigs mating. The gestation period for guinea pigs is between 62-68 days.

All too often, novices rush into breeding on a wave of enthusiasm and then lose interest when things do not go quite as they had anticipated. This is invariably because they were not adequately prepared and because the quality of their stock was just not good enough.

One of the great benefits of guinea pigs is that they have only small litters. This enables you to breed them at a low level and never be stuck with too many surplus babies. Often, there are friends who will be waiting for your youngsters if you have approached the matter on a planned build-up basis. Another great advantage to breeding these pets is that there is no waiting period to see what colors the babies will be. One night the mother-to-be will be very rotund; the next morning you will wake to see one or more babies scampering around the hutch or pen. Children love this aspect of guinea pigs.

◆ A Dalmatian guinea pig. This breed is named after the dog breed of the same name because of its black-and-white coloration.

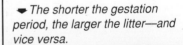

◆ The shorter the gestation period, the larger the litter—and vice versa.

Preparations

Once you have determined that you really want to be a breeder, you should start your preparations.

← *A good specimen will have a wide, blunt nose that allows for the eyes to be spaced widely apart.*

↓ *Female guinea pigs should be bred before they are six months of age; otherwise, problems can arise during delivery.*

← *A female guinea pig's first litter is usually her smallest. At birth, the babies are fully furred, and their eyes are open.*

Extra Housing: You will need three additional accommodations to the single guinea pig home that you already have. One will be to house the boar, one will be for young males, and one will be for young females. You will also need extra food bowls and water bottles, and more food and floor-covering materials than you might normally keep on hand.

Healthy Stock: You should be sure that your intended mates are in superb condition. Never breed an overweight sow, as this could result in problems. Never breed a sow or boar that is ill or that is recovering from an illness. Never breed any stock that displays malocclusion or other hereditary problems. Finally, never breed poor-quality stock because this does nothing at all for the future of the hobby.

If you presently have just one male or female, you should carefully consider whether either of them is worthy of being bred. Do you know the genetic base of their color pattern? If not, and if they are not very good examples of nicely marked and well built guinea pigs, it might be better to retain them as pets and buy a trio (one boar, two sows) of the breed, color, and pattern that you want . Alternatively (and better), you could use a breeder's stud boar on your sows, which will save you the cost of retaining a boar at this stage.

Breeding Facts

The limitation of space does not allow for an in-depth discussion of breeding in this book, so what follows are the basic facts of the subject. They will get you by, but you should make more detailed studies of the whole subject, depending on how extensive you want your breeding program to be.

Breeding Age: A sow should be bred before she is six months old if she is to be bred at all. After that age, her pelvic bones will become more rigid, and birthing problems could ensue. The boar matures more slowly, so he should be about six months of age or older before he is used. It is best to mate a young boar with an experienced sow, and vice versa.

A young sow can reach sexual maturity as early as four weeks of age. At about that time, she should be placed into the accommodations for females if the boar is left with her mother (which is not normally recommended). Young boars are capable of producing fertile sperm by the age of eight weeks; thus, when the young boars reach this age, they should be removed from the nursery pen and placed in the accommodations for males.

Estrus Cycle: This is the full period of time between one estrus and the next. In guinea pigs, it is within the range of 13-21 days, depending on the species. An average is 14-16 days. The actual period of heat during this cycle lasts for about 6-15 hours. It is during this time that the sow will allow the boar to mate her. She can be left in his pen for 30 days or less if a mating is observed.

Gestation: This is the time lapse between fertilization of the sow's eggs and the day the offspring are born. In guinea pigs, it ranges between 56-74 days, 62-68 being typical for the three species from which the domestic guinea pig is

During its first three to four weeks of life, a baby guinea pig will be sustained by its mother's milk.

If you do not have the time and resources required to properly raise a guinea pig family, you should not breed your guinea pig.

These youngsters are past the weaning stage and are now ready to go to their new homes.

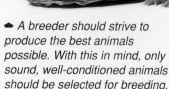

A breeder should strive to produce the best animals possible. With this in mind, only sound, well-conditioned animals should be selected for breeding.

probably descended. This is a long period of time; but keep in mind that the guinea pig, compared to other small mammals, is born in an advanced state of development.

Litter Size: The range is 1-13, and a typical litter will consist of four babies. Litter size is influenced by many factors, such as the age of the sow, the breeding strain, the health of the sow, the fecundity of the male, the ambient temperature at time of conception, and other factors. You might get only one or two babies, and in any litter there is always the chance that one or more youngsters will die shortly after being born.

Physical Appearance of the Young: Guinea pigs are born fully furred and with their eyes open. They are running around within hours of their birth. They can survive without their mother's milk from as young as five days of age, but this is neither normal nor recommended. They are able to eat solid foods within 24 hours of their birth.

Weaning Age: This is the time when young guinea pigs can live independent lives and are not being given milk by their mother. Weaning age is normally when the youngsters are 21 to 30 days old.

A female Abyssinian guinea pig.

Problems: The sow has only one pair of teats. If she has a large litter, this could present feeding problems. If more than five babies are born, it would be worth fostering them to a sow who has only 1-3 babies. If the sow is in a poor breeding state, she may not be able to release enough milk for her offspring, a situation

which, obviously, will be a problem. Seek veterinary help if the babies do not show obvious weight gains and a lot of activity.

Postpartum Mating: A sow will reenter estrus within hours of giving birth to a litter. This estrus will last for about 12 hours, which is ample time for the boar to mate her if he has been left with her. This is not recommended unless a colony system is in operation. It will weaken the sow and the resulting litter.

◄ At five months of age, these guinea pigs are fully mature.

◄ An agouti-and-white guinea pig. Guinea pigs are blunt and cobby in appearance.

➤ A tortoiseshell-and-white guinea pig. It is not easy to breed well-marked examples of this color variety.

➤ Bits of bedding and food particles can get entangled in the coats of the longhaired guinea pig varieties.

➤ A black guinea pig. In this variety, the color should be rich and deep and carried to the base of the skin.

Upper Breeding Age: A sow will usually cease breeding by the time she is about three years of age, or a little longer. By this time, the litter size will have become small in number. The boar's upper limit is not known but is certainly much longer than that of the sow, though his ability to implant fertile sperm will diminish with age.

Breeding Records

I suggest that you keep breeding records even if you practice only very limited breeding. For the regular breeder, records should be regarded as obligatory. The information on them will be very helpful in your future breeding plans. You can, of course, maintain very detailed records, the more the better; but as a minimum, the following should be regarded as basic: name or identification number of individuals mated; date of litter birth, number of offspring, and their sexes; their colors and patterns; how many of the litter survived to the age at which they could go to new homes; and notes on any kind of problems. Apart from the breeding records, you should also maintain individual cards on each guinea pig. The combined data on these cards can be used to determine future pairings as well as to trace any individuals that are passing on faults or problems. Additionally, it can be used to determine those that seem prepotent for their features.

Exhibition

Each country has its own rules for exhibition. Therefore, you should write to your national guinea pig society if the exhibition side of the hobby interests you. After you visit a few shows, you will soon become familiar with procedures.

In the USA, the following are the basic show classes and weights. A junior is a boar or sow not exceeding four months of age, and which has a weight range of 12-22 oz. An intermediate is up to six months of age and has a weight range of 22-32 oz. A senior boar or sow is any guinea pig weighing over 32 oz. The exhibits compete against each other on a comparison basis, but each variety and color does have a written standard of excellence drafted by the national guinea pig association. Classes are organized by age and weight, then by breed and variety (color), and, finally, by sex. In large shows, there will be more classes; whereas in small local affairs, a number of the colors or patterns may be in combined class form. Class winners compete against each other in a pyramid sort of manner so that ultimately there will be a Best in Show winner, the highest award given. A show guinea pig will, of course, need to be a very good example of its breed and color pattern.

★ Color and markings can vary considerably within a given litter.

★ A show guinea pig should be neither too fat nor too thin. Its coat must be in top condition.

◀ Even though baby guinea pigs are capable of eating solid food shortly after birth, it is highly recommended that they be allowed to nurse from their mother during their first few weeks of life.

↠ A guinea pig's claws should be checked monthly. If they become overly long, they should be clipped.

↟ Some guinea pig owners find it easier to first restrain their pet in a towel before clipping the claws.

↠ The more familiar you are with your guinea pig's behavior and habits, the easier it will be for you to determine when he is not feeling well.

Health Care

Over the many years that guinea pigs have been used for research purposes, it has been established that they are especially susceptible to antibiotic toxicity. For example, penicillin kills beneficial flora in the digestive system, thus allowing parasitic flora to multiply at the host's (the guinea pig's) expense. In such instances, guinea pigs can die within a matter of a few days following a rapid deterioration in their general health and appetite.

For these reasons, home diagnosis and treatment of illness should never be attempted. If you are ever concerned that your pet is unwell, do not delay. Discuss the problem immediately with your vet. Medication is often administered via the drinking water, but this presents its own problems. If the guinea pig does not drink enough, then the dosage will be too small and the risk of bacterial resistance will be greater. If the dosage is excessive, due to the daily addition of drugs to already treated water, then this, too, can be hazardous. Water must thus be supplied fresh each day and treated with the medication. When treating a sick guinea pig, you must isolate it so that its water intake is more readily monitored. At such times, greenfoods and fruit should be withheld (on your vet's advice) in order to encourage your pet to drink water. It is advisable to know your pet's weight because it will influence dosage.

↠ A pink-eyed white Abyssinian guinea pig.

Prevention is Best

Given the foregoing facts, you can see that it is altogether better to prevent disease than it is to treat it. While you can certainly study the diseases of guinea pigs and rodents in general, it is more useful to concentrate your efforts on hygiene and other aspects of husbandry. This is what we will focus on in this chapter.

It should be added that the pet owner with just one or two guinea pigs is at far less risk to diseases in his pets than the breeder-exhibitor who has a constant interchange of stock and who is often visiting many places where there could be a high risk of contracting diseases. The breeder must therefore be extra diligent in all husbandry techniques.

Hygiene

All food bowls must be cleaned on a daily basis, and they should always be returned to their respective cages—number the cages and the bowls. Replace any that become chipped or scratched to the point that

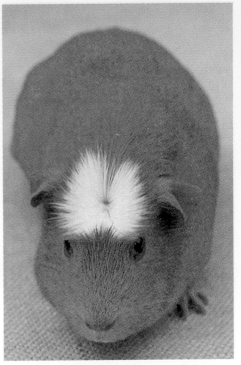

➤ White Crested American. Good husbandry is essential in maintaining a healthy guinea pig.

◀ You can supplement your guinea pig's diet with a number of fresh fruits and vegetables. Like people, guinea pigs can vary in their tastes.

A Silkie. In this breed, the long hair does not cover the face. Additionally, there is no part in the hair on the middle of the back.

After a bath, a guinea pig must be thoroughly dried to prevent it from getting chilled.

This Peruvian guinea pig was photographed during a break at a show. The crowning glory of this breed is its long hair.

they are not readily cleaned. Water bottles should be cleaned at a minimum of once a week. The same applies to the cages or other accommodations. Be extra attentive to the cage corners, where bacteria can easily build up.

Housing should be routinely painted each year. Ideally, it is also wise to have a number of spare pens or cages so that all housing periodically goes through a phase in which it can be thoroughly disinfected, rinsed, and allowed to remain empty. Floors, walls, and ceilings of breeding rooms should also be washed each week.

The breeder must ensure that ventilation is good because many problems stem from lack of fresh air and the rapid build-up of airborne bacteria. The use of an ionizer in the stock room will help keep dust and, thus, bacteria to a low level. Ionizers are available in numerous capacities from pet shops.

Always wash your hands

before and after handling your pets, especially so if any are unwell. Never "store" dirtied floor-covering near your stock—dispose of it as soon as the cages are cleaned.

It will certainly be useful if light-sensitive dimmer switches are installed in the breeding room. Failing this, automatic light-timers or the use of low-wattage night lights is recommended.

Minor Cuts

If your pet should be cut in a fight or by accident, the wound should first be cleaned with a mild saline solution and then treated with an antiseptic powder or lotion, which will reduce the possibility of secondary infection. Deep lacerations must be treated by your vet.

Isolation

If a guinea pig is suspected of being ill, it should be isolated from its cagemates as soon as possible. Keep it in a comfortably warm environment, which will usually help to overcome minor conditions brought about by chilling. If numerous clinical signs of ill health are seen, contact your vet.

← A healthy guinea pig will have bright clear eyes and a dry nose. The inside of the ears will be clean and free of any foreign matter.

← Regular dental checkups are another important aspect of your pet's preventive health care. If the teeth become too long, they should be clipped. You can ask your vet to do this for you.

◀ The long hair of the Peruvian must be put up in wrappers to prevent it from getting soiled. Wrappers can be fashioned from small pieces of soft cloth.

Whether purebred or mixed breed, guinea pigs are generally hardy animals.

Quarantine

All breeders should have quarantine quarters well away from their main stock. Quarantine quarters allow any incubating illnesses to manifest themselves during the isolation period, which should be 14-21 days. Remember that when a guinea pig moves to a new home, this alone will

Many of the health problems in guinea pigs can be traced to improper care on the part of the owner. As is true for the maintenance of other kinds of pets, an ounce of prevention is worth a pound of cure.

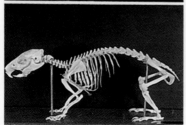

create stress and can cause initial problems. Stress is a major precursor of disease, which is why quarantining is so important to the breeder-exhibitor.

With a fair amount of common sense on your part, good feeding, and spacious accommodations, your pet guinea pig hopefully will not experience any undue problems.

Skeletal specimen of a guinea pig. Members of this species have a very stocky build.

Which Breed and Variety?

There are eleven breeds of cavy from which you can choose, these breeds being determined by their coat type. Within the breeds, there is a wide variety of beautiful colors and patterns. Some color patterns are not as easily obtained in a given coat type as are others. They may simply be less popular, or they may not yet have been well established. There are many other permutations of coat type and color that are possible, and no doubt they will appear in the coming years.

The standards of the US and Britain do differ, both in their descriptions and in what is acceptable in certain breeds, e.g., in the crested varieties. The following is a general guide that will be quite adequate for the pet owner. The potential breeder-exhibitor should be familiar with the standards as they apply in his own country.

← This guinea pig has very unusual face markings. It was bred by a breeder in Europe.

▶ Grass is fine as an occasional treat. Just be sure that it has not been contaminated by pesticides or other kinds of chemicals.

◄ The cream coloration of this guinea pig is rather uneven. While it might not do very well on the show bench, it can still make a fine pet.

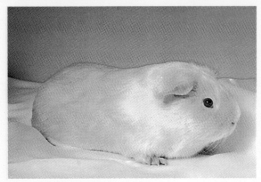

← A lovely lilac guinea pig. For the first-time owner, it is a good idea to start with a shorthaired guinea pig, which is easier to care for than one of the longhaired varieties.

The Breeds

The oldest coat types are the smoothcoated, the Abyssinian, and the Peruvian. Each of them is also seen in a satin finish. The smoothcoated is known in the US as the American, but it is the same breed as the smoothcoated, or self, of Britain. The Abyssinian has a harsh coat in which the fur is arranged in a pattern of rosettes. In a quality guinea pig, the rosettes should be placed in a definite manner.

The Peruvian is longhaired, the fur reaching over 50cm (20 in.) in a good exhibition specimen. This breed is certainly not recommended for the pet owner just starting out in guinea pigs because of the amount of time and problems encountered in maintaining the coat. It can, of course, be regularly trimmed to a more practical length.

← When introducing a new food to your guinea pig, do so gradually to prevent digestive problems.

↑ These children let their guinea pigs play in an outdoor hutch when the weather is nice. Guinea pigs should not be left unattended in such a structure because they can be frightened or possibly harmed by stray animals.

Similar to the Peruvian is the Silkie, which is known as the Sheltie in Britain. It differs from the other longhaired variety in that there is no long hair over the face. Additionally, there is no part in the hair over the middle of the back.

Of more recent origin is the Teddy, or Rex, as it is called in Britain. In this breed, the guard hairs are very short, creating a very unique texture. The White Crested sports a rosette on the crown of its head. This rosette should radiate evenly from its center. Breeding perfect White Cresteds is more difficult than breeding colored cresteds. In the US, the crest is white and this is the only white allowed in the breed. You cannot (for show purposes) have a white-crested Dutch, Hima-

▲ The color markings of this Silkie are predominantly agouti.

layan, or any other pattern that includes white in it. In Britain, the crest can match the body color, meaning it does not have to be white. Therefore, it is simply a crested breed.

The satin is not a breed per se but creates one by being added to the basic coat type. For example, the fur of a smoothcoated guinea pig has a fine sheen to it. When the satin mutation is present, the fur appears super glossy or satin-like.

◀ Guinea pigs cannot manufacture their own vitamin C. Therefore they have to obtain it from an outside source. There are many fruits and vegetables that contain this important vitamin.

◆ A hand-tame youngster. A guinea pig handled from a young age can make a good, tractable pet.

Colors and Patterns

The wild-color pattern of the guinea pig is known as agouti. It

comprises shafts of hair banded in black, brown, and yellow. The arrangement of the three colors create what is known as a "ticked" effect. With the passing of time, many mutations have appeared, especially during this century. They have been retained and selectively improved to produce the present impressive range of possibilities. There have been a number of alterations to the agouti pattern itself, which can be seen in about fourteen different forms.

Colors can be broadly broken down into selfs and non-selfs. A self is a single-color guinea pig. At once I must also add that in Britain, a self, without further qualification, is also a fur type, in this instance being a shortcoated guinea pig. A Peruvian or Abyssinian can be a self color but is not exhibited in self classes. The self colors are black, blue, chocolate, lilac, beige, cream, red, red-eyed orange, golden, red-eyed white, and albino. Alternative names for some of these colors may by used on either side of the Atlantic. The true albino is devoid of any color pigment and should be distinguished from white, in which some pigment is evident in the ears. The potential for colors within the red to cream range is almost unlimited; there is one for every taste.

The non-selfs will include all guinea pigs displaying two or more colors.

☛ T.F.H. Publications offers the most comprehensive selection of books dealing with guinea pigs. A selection of significant titles is presented below; they and many other works are available from your local pet shop.